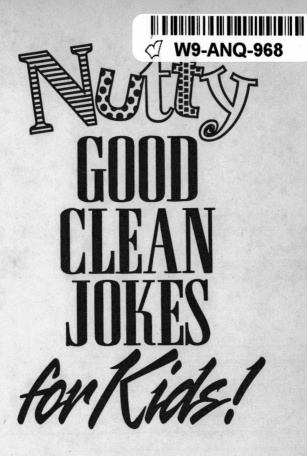

Nutty GOOD CLEAN JOKES for Kids!

BOB PHILLIPS

HARVEST HOUSE PUBLISHERS
Eugene, Oregon 97402

Scripture quotations in this book are taken from the King James Version of the Bible.

NUTTY GOOD CLEAN JOKES FOR KIDS

Copyright © 1995 by Harvest House Publishers
Eugene, Oregon 97402

ISBN 1-56507-374-6

Printed in the United States of America.

95 96 97 98 99 00 — 10 9 8 7 6 5 4 3 2

To the
Notorious, novel, neat, nice, and nutty
Nunziato family

Contents

1

Willard & Wallace

Willard: What question do you always have to answer by saying Yes?
Wallace: I have no clue.
Willard: What does *y-e-s* spell?

Willard: Why do eggs go to the gym?
Wallace: Beats me.
Willard: They like to Eggsercise.

Willard: If you wanted to take a bath without water, what would you do?

Wallace: I can't guess.
Willard: Take a sunbath.

❖　❖　❖

Willard: What happens to a person who lies down in front of a car?
Wallace: I have no idea.
Willard: He gets tired.

❖　❖　❖

Willard: What did the nylons say to the garter belt?
Wallace: You tell me.
Willard: Make it snappy. We've gotta run.

❖　❖　❖

Willard: What goes tick-tock-woof?
Wallace: I give up.
Willard: A watchdog.

❖　❖　❖

Willard: What kinds of birds are kept in captivity more than any others?
Wallace: Who knows?
Willard: Jailbirds.

❖ ❖ ❖

Willard: What is both small and large at the same time?
Wallace: You've got me.
Willard: A jumbo shrimp.

❖ ❖ ❖

Willard: What kind of a bone should you not give to a dog?
Wallace: My mind is blank.
Willard: A trombone.

❖ ❖ ❖

Willard: What do you call a hot dog when it's in a bad mood?
Wallace: That's a mystery.
Willard: A crank-furter.

2

Bible Questions & Answers

What are two of the smallest insects mentioned in the Bible?

The widow's "mites" and the "wicked flee"—Mark 12:42 and Proverbs 28:1.

Who is the smallest man mentioned in the Bible?

Some people believe that it was Zacchaeus. Others believe it was Nehemiah (Knee-high-a-miah), or Bildad, the Shuhite (Shoe-height). But in reality it was Peter the disciple. He slept on his watch.

One of the first things Cain did after he left the Garden of Eden was to take a nap. How do we know this?

Because he went to the land of Nod—Genesis 4:16.

Where is the second math problem mentioned in the Bible?

When God told Adam and Eve to go forth and multiply—Genesis 1:28.

Where is the first math problem mentioned in the Bible?

When God divided the light from the darkness—Genesis 1:4.

Who was the first person in the Bible to eat herself out of house and home?

Eve.

❖ ❖ ❖

12

Who was the straightest man in the Bible?

Joseph. Pharaoh made a ruler out of him.

If Methuselah was the oldest man in the Bible (969 years of age), why did he die before his father?

His father was Enoch. Enoch never died; he walked with God—Genesis 5:24.

Who introduced the first walking stick?

Eve . . . when she presented Adam with a little Cain.

Why was Moses the most wicked man in the Bible?

Because he broke the Ten Commandments all at once.

Was there any money on Noah's ark?

Yes. The duck took a bill, the frog took a greenback, and the skunk took a scent.

Where in the Bible does it say that fathers should let their sons use the automobile?

In Proverbs 13:24—"He that spareth his rod hateth his son."

3

Debby & Denise

Debby: What do they call the man who cuts the lion's hair?
Denise: I have no clue.
Debby: The mane man.

❖   ❖   ❖

Debby: If you were invited out to dinner and found nothing on the table but a beet, what would you say?
Denise: I haven't the foggiest.
Debby: Well, that beet's all!

❖   ❖   ❖

Debby: They were planning to add my brother's head to Mount Rushmore.

Denise: What happened?

Debby: They couldn't find rock that was thick enough.

Debby: I went to my doctor and told him I was having trouble breathing.

Denise: Really? What did he say?

Debby: He told me he could give me something to stop it.

Debby: Do you like your job cleaning chimneys?

Denise: It certainly soots me.

Debby: Is it true that pigs make good drivers?

Denise: I hear that they're road hogs.

Debby: Denise, I don't like the cheese with holes in it.

Denise: Okay, just eat the cheese and leave the holes on the side of your plate.

Debby: My ancestors came over on the Mayflower.

Denise: My ancestors came over a month before—on the April Shower.

Debby: I just love to be in the country and hear the trees whisper.

Denise: That may be okay, but I hate to hear the grass mown.

4

Nit & Wit

Nit: What do you say to a tailor about his clothes?
Wit: I have no clue.
Nit: Suit yourself.

❖ ❖ ❖

Nit: What do you say to a guy driving a car with no engine?
Wit: Beats me.
Nit: How's it going?

❖ ❖ ❖

Nit: What did they do to the lady who stole

some eye makeup?

Wit: I can't guess.

Nit: She got 50 lashes.

❖ ❖ ❖

Nit: What's red and red and red all over?

Wit: I have no idea.

Nit: Measles with a sunburn.

❖ ❖ ❖

Nit: Did you hear about the camper who swallowed the flashlight?

Wit: That's awful.

Nit: Yeah, he hiccuped with de-light.

❖ ❖ ❖

Nit: What did the wise old canary say to the parrot?

Wit: I give up.

Nit: Talk is cheap-cheap.

❖ ❖ ❖

Nit: What is the other name for TV soap operas?

Wit: Who knows?

Nit: Dope operas.

Nit: What do you call a bee that talks in very low tones?
Wit: You've got me.
Nit: A mumble-bee.

Nit: What do you get if you cross a porcupine with a peacock?
Wit: My mind is blank.
Nit: A sharp dresser.

Nit: What do you get when you cross a motor-cycle with a jokebook?
Wit: That's a mystery.
Nit: A yamahaha.

Nit: What do bank robbers like to eat with their soup?
Wit: I don't know.
Nit: Safe crackers.

5

Who's There?

Knock, knock.
Who's there?
Annie.
Annie who?
Annie body home?

❖ ❖ ❖

Knock, knock.
Who's there?
Wooden shoe.
Wooden shoe who?
Wooden shoe like to know!

❖ ❖ ❖

Knock, knock.
Who's there?
Noah.
Noah who?
Noah good knock-knock joke?

❖　❖　❖

Knock, knock.
Who's there?
Catsup.
Catsup who?
Catsup a tree. Quick, call the fire department!

❖　❖　❖

Knock, knock.
Who's there?
Huron.
Huron who?
Huron time for once.

❖　❖　❖

Knock, knock.
Who's there?
Foreign.
Foreign who?
Foreign 20 blackbirds baked in a pie.

❖　❖　❖

Knock, knock.
Who's there?
Cain.
Cain who?
Cain you hear me going knock, knock?

❖　❖　❖

Knock, knock.
Who's there?
BeeHive.
BeeHive who?
BeeHive yourself or you will get into trouble.

❖　❖　❖

Knock, knock.
Who's there?
Mack.
Mack who?
Mack up your mind.

❖　❖　❖

Knock, knock.
Who's there?
Pasteur.
Pasteur who?
It's Pasteur bedtime.

❖　❖　❖

Knock, knock.
Who's there?
WashOut.
WashOut who?
WashOut, I'm coming in!

6

Fred & Ted

Fred: What is the best way to introduce a hamburger?
Ted: I have no clue.
Fred: Meat Patty.

❖ ❖ ❖

Fred: What does the Lone Ranger's horse eat with?
Ted: Beats me.
Fred: Silverware.

❖ ❖ ❖

Fred: What does a pheasant say when it

kisses its children good night?

Ted: I can't guess.

Fred: Pheasant dreams.

Fred: What would you get if you crossed a nut and a briefcase?

Ted: I have no idea.

Fred: A nut case.

Fred: What did one earthquake say to the other earthquake?

Ted: You tell me.

Fred: It's all your fault.

Fred: What do you get if you cross a peacock with an insect?

Ted: I give up.

Fred: A cocky roach.

Fred: What's the best kind of trousers for a wise guy to wear?

Ted: Who knows?

Fred: Smarty-pants.

❖ ❖ ❖

Fred: What do you call a contented rabbit?
Ted: You've got me.
Fred: Hoppy-go-lucky.

❖ ❖ ❖

Fred: What happens if you swallow a frog?
Ted: My mind is blank.
Fred: You'll probably croak any minute.

7

Lisa & Lucile

Lisa: What did Humpty-Dumpty die of?
Lucile: I have no clue.
Lisa: Shell shock.

Lisa: What's the difference between a knight in shining armor and Rudolph the red-nosed Reindeer?
Lucile: Beats me.
Lisa: One is a dragon slayer, and the other is a sleigh dragger.

Lisa: What happened to the guy who stole one thousand Three Musketeer candy bars?

Lucile: I can't guess.

Lisa: He ended up behind bars.

❖ ❖ ❖

Lisa: How did one cactus compliment another cactus?

Lucile: I have no idea.

Lisa: You look sharp today.

❖ ❖ ❖

Lisa: What did one garbage can say to the other garbage can?

Lucile: You tell me.

Lisa: Nothing. Garbage cans can't talk.

❖ ❖ ❖

Lisa: What do you call a Texan who moves to Alaska?

Lucile: I give up.

Lisa: A traitor.

❖ ❖ ❖

Lisa: What happened when the skunk wrote a novel?

Lucile: Who knows?
Lisa: It became a best-smeller.

❖ ❖ ❖

Lisa: What is the favorite kind of cake for policemen?
Lucile: You've got me.
Lisa: Copcakes.

❖ ❖ ❖

Lisa: What is black and white and yellow?
Lucile: My mind is blank.
Lisa: A bus full of zebras.

❖ ❖ ❖

Lisa: What restaurants do slow-moving snails avoid?
Lucile: That's a mystery.
Lisa: Fast-food places.

8

Jon-Mark & Jonas

Jon-Mark: Jonas, your hands are very dirty. What would you say if I came to your house with dirty hands?

Jonas: I'd be too polite to mention it.

Jon-Mark: Jonas! What is this fly doing in the alphabet soup you gave me?

Jonas: Learning to read.

Jon-Mark: This goulash is terrible.

Jonas: That's funny. I put a brand-new pair of goulashes in it.

❖   ❖   ❖

Jon-Mark: You mean to tell me that you've lived in this out-of-the-way town for more than 25 years? I can't see what there is here to keep you busy.

Jonas: There isn't anything to keep me busy. That's why I like it!

❖   ❖   ❖

Jon-Mark: I have eight eyes, four legs, six eyebrows, webbed fingers, and my purple hair stands straight up. What am I?

Jonas: Something very ugly.

❖   ❖   ❖

Jon-Mark: My dog has no nose. How does he smell?

Jonas: Who knows?

Jon-Mark: Awful.

❖   ❖   ❖

Jon-Mark: If you were in line at a train ticket window and the man in front of you was going to Los Angeles and the lady in back of you was going to Florida, where would you be going?

Jonas: You've got me.

Jon-Mark: If you don't know, then what are you doing in line?

Jon-Mark: Can you tell me where hippos are found?

Jonas: Hippos are so big that they hardly ever get lost.

Jon-Mark: Imagine meeting you here at the psychiatrist's office! Are you coming or going?

Jonas: If I knew that, I wouldn't be here!

Jonas: I'll bet my name is harder than yours.

Jon-Mark: All right, what's your name?

Jonas: Stone.

Jon-Mark: You lose. My name is Harder.

9

Did You Hear?

Did you hear about the absentminded train conductor?

He lost track of things.

Did you hear about the deck chair factories that lost money?

They folded.

Did you hear about the sword swallower who worked for nothing?

He was a free-lancer.

34

Did you hear about the absentminded musician?

He had to leave himself notes.

Did you hear about the cowboy who fell in the leaves?

He was accused of rustling.

Did you hear the joke about the mountain climber?

He hasn't made it up yet.

Did you hear about the weatherman who went back to college?

He got several degrees.

Did you hear about the weatherman who won the race?

He said it was a breeze.

Did you hear about the glue truck that over-turned?

Police were asking motorists to stick to their own lanes.

Did you hear about the investigator who joined the army?

He was a private eye.

Did you hear about the accident at the string-bean factory?

Two workers got canned.

Did you hear about the knitting needle that told jokes?

It could keep you in stitches.

Bill & Jill

Bill: Why did the elephant paint his toes white?
Jill: I have no clue.
Bill: So he could hide in a bag of marsh-mallows.

Bill: Why did the clock have to go to the mental hospital?
Jill: Beats me.
Bill: It was a little cuckoo.

37

Bill: Why do pickles laugh when you touch them?
Jill: I can't guess.
Bill: They're pickle-ish.

Bill: Why is a vacuum cleaner like a gossip?
Jill: I have no idea.
Bill: Because it picks up lots of dirt.

Bill: Why isn't the elderly female mayor getting reelected?
Jill: You tell me.
Bill: Because the old gray mayor ain't what she used to be.

❖ ❖ ❖

Bill: Why did the nutty kid put his head on the grindstone?
Jill: I give up.
Bill: To sharpen his wits.

❖ ❖ ❖

Bill: Want to know why I stopped going to the masseur?

Jill: Sure, tell me.
Bill: He rubbed me the wrong way.

Bill: Why is it so easy to find a lost elephant?
Jill: You've got me.
Bill: It has the odor of peanuts on its breath.

Bill: Why do carpenters and plumbers write on sandpaper?
Jill: My mind is blank.
Bill: They like to give rough estimates.

Bill: Why does a hippopotamus wear glasses?
Jill: That's a mystery.
Bill: So he can read fine print.

Bill: Why did the optometrist and his wife have an argument?
Jill: I don't know.
Bill: They couldn't see eye to eye.

Bible Riddles

Who was the best financier in the Bible?

Noah. He floated his stock while the whole world was in liquidation.

Where does it talk about Honda cars in the Bible?

In Acts 1:14: "These all continued with one accord."

40

What prophet in the Bible was a space traveler?

Elijah. He went up in a fiery chariot—2 Kings 2:11.

What city in the Bible was named after something that you find on every modern-day car?

Tyre.

When the ark landed on Mount Ararat, was Noah the first one out?

No, he came forth out of the ark.

Which one of Noah's sons was considered to be a clown?

His second son. He was always a Ham.

Which came first—the chicken or the egg?

The chicken, of course. God doesn't lay any eggs.

Why didn't they play cards on Noah's ark?
Because Noah sat on the deck.

Where was deviled ham mentioned in the Bible?
When the evil spirits entered the swine.

What man in the Bible spoke when he was a very small baby?
Job. He cursed the day he was born.

What did Noah say while he was loading all the animals on the Ark?
Now I herd everything.

What was the first theatrical event in the Bible?
Eve's appearance for Adam's benefit.

Ryan & Reginald

Ryan: What do you sell?
Reginald: Salt.
Ryan: I'm a salt seller, too.
Reginald: Shake.

❖ ❖ ❖

Ryan: What does an egg get when it does too much work?
Reginald: Beats me.
Ryan: Eggs-hausted.

❖ ❖ ❖

Ryan: What do you get if you cross a hippopotamus with a cat?

Reginald: I can't guess.
Ryan: A hippopotamus with nine lives.

Ryan: What belongs to you and yet is used by other people more often than by yourself?
Reginald: I have no idea.
Ryan: Your name.

Ryan: What kind of vehicles do hitch hikers like to ride in?
Reginald: You tell me.
Ryan: Pickup trucks.

Ryan: What happens when you stand behind a car?
Reginald: I give up.
Ryan: You get exhausted.

Ryan: What city are you in when you drop your waffle in the sand?
Reginald: Who knows?
Ryan: Sandy Eggo.

❖   ❖   ❖

Ryan: What do you call a little bird at the stereo shop?
Reginald: You've got me.
Ryan: A tweeter.

❖   ❖   ❖

Ryan: What do you call it when your brother has a brainstorm?
Reginald: My mind is blank.
Ryan: Drizzle.

❖   ❖   ❖

Ryan: What do surgeons charge their patients?
Reginald: That's a mystery.
Ryan: Cut rates.

13

Rex & Tex

Rex: What did one closet say to the other closet?
Tex: I have no clue.
Rex: Clothes the door.

❖ ❖ ❖

Rex: What animal eats the least?
Tex: Beats me.
Rex: The moth. It just eats holes.

❖ ❖ ❖

Rex: What do you call a hen that cracks jokes?

Tex: I can't guess.
Rex: A comedi-hen.

Rex: What do you say to a liar at the dinner table?
Tex: I have no idea.
Rex: Pass the baloney.

Rex: What did one needle say to another needle?
Tex: You tell me.
Rex: Sew tell me, what's new?

Rex: What did the astronauts say when they found bones on the moon?
Tex: I give up.
Rex: I guess the cow didn't make it.

Rex: What does an odd fellow do when he tries to get revenge?
Tex: Who knows?
Rex: He tries to get even.

Rex: What do you get if you cross a potato with a beet?

Tex: You've got me.

Rex: A potato with bloodshot eyes.

Rex: What happened to the guy who picked a fight at the shopping center?

Tex: My mind is blank.

Rex: He was malled.

Rex: What would you get if you crossed some pasta with a boa constrictor?

Tex: That's a mystery.

Rex: Spaghetti that winds itself around your fork.

Rex: What part of the Bible do people who love math read?

Tex: I don't know.

Rex: The book of Numbers.

14

Calvin & Cora

Calvin: What is the name of the person who brings gifts to the dentist's office?
Cora: I have no clue.
Calvin: Santa Floss.

Calvin: What do you think a Laplander is?
Cora: Beats me.
Calvin: Someone who can't keep his balance while riding on a bus.

Calvin: It's Washington's birthday, so I baked

you a cherry pie.

Cora: All right, bring me a hatchet so I can cut it.

Calvin: Abraham Lincoln once dined at this very table in my house.

Cora: Is that why you haven't changed the tablecloth since?

Calvin: If a man was locked up in a room with only a bat and a piano, how could he get out?

Cora: You tell me.

Calvin: There are two ways: He could swing the bat three times for an out, or use a piano key.

Calvin: My brother just opened a candy business.

Cora: Is he doing well?

Calvin: So far he's made a mint.

Calvin: I had a wrestler friend who didn't feel

well so he went to the doctor.

Cora: What did the doctor say?

Calvin: He told him to get a grip on himself.

Calvin: I wrote a letter to Dear Abby. This is what I said—"Dear Abby: Is it good manners to answer a question with just a single word? Signed, Polite."

Cora: Did she write back?

Calvin: Yes. This is what she said to me—"Dear Polite: No."

Calvin: I would like to go on a boat trip, but I can't afford it.

Cora: I know. Beggars can't be cruisers.

Calvin: Do moths cry?

Cora: That's a mystery.

Calvin: Yes. Haven't you ever seen a moth bawl?

15

Lydia & Larry

Lydia: What did the comedian say to the cattle rancher?
Larry: I have no clue.
Lydia: Herd any good ones lately?

Lydia: What did Adam say to Eve on the night of December 24?
Larry: Beats me.
Lydia: Is this Christmas, Eve?

Lydia: What game do you play with bees?

Larry: I can't guess.
Lydia: Hive and seek.

Lydia: What do they call a young rabbit that never goes outside the house?
Larry: I have no idea.
Lydia: An ingrown hare.

Lydia: How can you tell the difference between the land and the ocean?
Larry: You tell me.
Lydia: The land is dirty and the ocean is tide-y.

Lydia: What entertainment did Noah hire for the animals?
Larry: I give up.
Lydia: An ark-estra.

Lydia: What did Mary order when she went out for dinner?
Larry: Who knows?

Lydia: Everybody knows that Mary had a little lamb.

Lydia: What did the duck say to Jack Frost?
Larry: You've got me.
Lydia: How about a quacker, Jack?

Lydia: What do you get when you cross Moby Dick and a Timex wrist watch?
Larry: My mind is blank.
Lydia: A whale watch-er.

Lydia: What did the nutty guy say when he saw a bowl of Cheerios?
Larry: That's a mystery.
Lydia: Look—doughnut seeds!

Lydia: What did the sock say to the needle?
Larry: I don't know.
Lydia: I'll be darned!

16

Jeff & Joel

Jeff: What do you call a horse that never stops telling you what to do?

Joel: I have no clue.

Jeff: A real nag.

❖ ❖ ❖

Jeff: What seems to be your trouble?

Joel: After I get up in the morning, I'm always dizzy for half an hour.

Jeff: Then why don't you get up half an hour later?

❖ ❖ ❖

Jeff: What did George Washington say to his men before crossing the Delaware?

Joel: I can't guess.

Jeff: Get in the boat.

❖ ❖ ❖

Jeff: What did the jelly bean say to the Milky Way bar?

Joel: I have no idea.

Jeff: Smile, you're on candied camera.

❖ ❖ ❖

Jeff: What's the cure for Monday-morning blues?

Joel: You tell me.

Jeff: Tuesday.

❖ ❖ ❖

Jeff: What kind of monkey flies?

Joel: I give up.

Jeff: A hot-air baboon.

❖ ❖ ❖

Jeff: What do ducks eat for breakfast?

Joel: Who knows?

Jeff: Quacker Oats.

❖ ❖ ❖

Jeff: What do you say to a crying whale?
Joel: You've got me.
Jeff: Quit your blubbering.

❖ ❖ ❖

Jeff: What is a mosquito's favorite sport?
Joel: My mind is blank.
Jeff: Skin diving.

❖ ❖ ❖

Jeff: What happened on the Fourth of July?
Joel: That's a mystery.
Jeff: I don't know. I'm not good at fractions.

17

Open the Door

Knock, knock.
Who's there?
Cows go.
Cows go who?
No, cows go "moo."

❖ ❖ ❖

Knock, knock.
Who's there?
Howell.
Howell who?
Howell I get in if you don't open the door?

❖ ❖ ❖

Knock, knock.
Who's there?
Abbey.
Abbey who?
Abbey birthday.

❖ ❖ ❖

Knock, knock.
Who's there?
Police.
Police who?
Police stop telling me these nutty knock-knock jokes!

❖ ❖ ❖

Knock, knock.
Who's there?
Freeze.
Freeze who?
Freeze a jolly good fellow . . .

❖ ❖ ❖

Knock, knock.
Who's there?
Henrietta.
Henrietta who?
Henrietta worm that was in his apple.

❖ ❖ ❖

Knock, knock.
Who's there?
Annapolis.
Annapolis who?
Annapolis day keeps the doctor away.

❖ ❖ ❖

Knock, knock.
Who's there?
Adam.
Adam who?
Adam my way, I'm coming in!

❖ ❖ ❖

Knock, knock.
Who's there?
Kenya.
Kenya who?
Kenya hear me knocking?

❖ ❖ ❖

Knock, knock.
Who's there?
Midas.
Midas who?
Midas well try again.

18

Edgar & Emily

Edgar: What is the recipe to make a chocolate drop?

Emily: I have no clue.

Edgar: Let it fall from your hand.

❖ ❖ ❖

Edgar: How did the police describe the hitch-hiker?

Emily: Beats me.

Edgar: They gave a thumbnail description.

❖ ❖ ❖

Edgar: How did the farmer count his cows?

Emily: I can't guess.
Edgar: He used a cow-culator.

Edgar: How is the monogram business you started?
Emily: I've had some initial success.

Edgar: How did your dog get a new apartment?
Emily: You tell me.
Edgar: He signed a leash.

Edgar: What is the best way find a math tutor?
Emily: I give up.
Edgar: Place an add.

Edgar: How much did the polar bear weigh?
Emily: Who knows?
Edgar: A ton-dra.

Edgar: How do you make a skeleton laugh?
Emily: You've got me.
Edgar: Tickle its funny bone.

❖ ❖ ❖

Edgar: How do you glue your mouth shut?
Emily: My mind is blank.
Edgar: With lipstick.

❖ ❖ ❖

Edgar: Did you like the carnival?
Emily: Oh, I don't know.
Edgar: Well, I thought it was fair.

❖ ❖ ❖

Edgar: How can you tell when there's a mosquito in your bed?
Emily: I don't know.
Edgar: By the M on its pajamas.

19

Bible Fun

Who was the first man in the Bible to know the meaning of rib roast?

Adam.

On the ark, Noah probably got milk from the cows. What did he get from the ducks?

Quackers.

What was the difference between the 10,000 soldiers of Israel and the 300 soldiers Gideon chose for battle?

9700.

64

Certain days in the Bible passed by more quickly than most of the days. Which days were these?

The fast days.

Matthew and Mark have something that is not found in Luke and John. What is it?

The letter a.

In the story of the good Samaritan, why did the Levite pass by on the other side?

Because the poor man had already been robbed.

At what season of the year did Eve eat the fruit?

Early in the fall.

What has God never seen, Abraham Lincoln

seldom saw, and today's man sees every day?

His equal—Isaiah 40:25.

Where is medicine first mentioned in the Bible?
Where the Lord gives Moses two tablets.

Where does it say in the Bible that we should not fly in airplanes?

In Matthew 28:20—"Lo, I am with you always."

Where in the Bible does it talk about smoking?

In Genesis 24:64—Rebekah "lighted off the camel."

20

Christy & Quentin

Christy: I love to cook breakfast for my friends. Is it proper for me to cook it in my pajamas?

Quentin: It's not improper, but it can be a big mess. I would recommend trying a frying pan.

Christy: You never seem to age. I wonder if you can tell me how I could avoid getting wrinkles.

Quentin: Beats me.

Christy: Maybe I should stop sleeping in my clothes.

❖ ❖ ❖

Christy: Did you hear about the golfer?
Quentin: No, I didn't. What about him?
Christy: He joined a club.

❖ ❖ ❖

Christy: I'm studying to be a barber.
Quentin: Will it take long?
Christy: No, I'm learning all the shortcuts

❖ ❖ ❖

Christy: Well, Quentin, how do you like school?
Quentin: Closed!

❖ ❖ ❖

Christy: Did you get hurt when you fell and struck the piano?
Quentin: No, I hit the soft pedal.

❖ ❖ ❖

Christy: Will your dog eat off my hand?
Quentin: Yes, and he will eat off your leg, too.

Christy: Mississippi is a very long word, but I can spell it.

Quentin: Okay, spell it.

Christy: I-T.

❖ ❖ ❖

Christy: Is there any difference between lightning and electricity?

Quentin: Yes. You don't have to pay for lightning.

❖ ❖ ❖

Christy: Did you hear about the Texas millionaire whose wife was sick?

Quentin: No, what happened?

Christy: He walked into the Cadillac salesroom and said, "My wife has a touch of the flu. Do you have anything in the way of a get-well car?"

21

Arnold & Amy

Arnold: Why does a frog have more lives than a cat?
Amy: I have no clue.
Arnold: Because it croaks every night.

Arnold: Why did the baseball player go to the store?
Amy: Beats me.
Arnold: For a sales pitch.

Arnold: Why did the class clown give a smart

girl a dog biscuit?
Amy: I can't guess.
Arnold: He heard she was the teacher's pet.

Arnold: Why did the bee go to the doctor?
Amy: I have no idea.
Arnold: It had hives.

Arnold: Why was the plumber so tired?
Amy: You tell me.
Arnold: He felt drained.

Arnold: Why did the pinky go to jail?
Amy: I give up.
Arnold: He was fingered by the police.

Arnold: Why did the bird always like to sit down?
Amy: Who knows?
Arnold: He was a stool pigeon.

Arnold: Why did the nutty boy lock his father in the refrigerator?

Amy: You've got me.

Arnold: Because he wanted a cold pop.

Arnold: Why did the turkey cross the road?

Amy: My mind is blank.

Arnold: Because the chicken retired and moved to Florida.

Arnold: Why did the cottage go on a diet?

Amy: That's a mystery.

Arnold: It wanted to be a lighthouse.

Arnold: Why are you shivering, Amy?

Amy: I guess it must be this zero on my test paper.

22

Doreen & Duncan

Doreen: Why did the kangaroo go to the psychiatrist?
Duncan: I have no clue.
Doreen: Because it was jumpy.

❖ ❖ ❖

Doreen: Why don't elephants dance?
Duncan: Beats me.
Doreen: Nobody ever asks them.

❖ ❖ ❖

Doreen: Why is noodle soup good for you?
Duncan: I can't guess.

Doreen: Because it's brain food.

Doreen: Why did the runner bring his barber to the Olympics?
Duncan: I have no idea.
Doreen: He wanted to shave a few seconds off his time.

Doreen: Why does it take so long to make a politician snowman?
Duncan: You tell me.
Doreen: You have to hollow out the head first.

Doreen: Why didn't the weatherman ever get tired?
Duncan: I give up.
Doreen: He always got a second wind.

Doreen: Why do chickens think cooks are mean?
Duncan: Who knows?
Doreen: They beat eggs.

❖ ❖ ❖

Doreen: Why did the bubble gum cross the road?

Duncan: You've got me.

Doreen: It was stuck to the chicken's foot.

❖ ❖ ❖

Doreen: Why is it hard to carry on a conversation with a goat?

Duncan: My mind is blank.

Doreen: It's always butting in.

❖ ❖ ❖

Doreen: Why don't ducks tell jokes while they are flying?

Duncan: That's a mystery.

Doreen: Because they would quack up.

Doreen: Why did it take so long for the elephant to cross the road?

Duncan: I don't know.

Doreen: Because the chicken had trouble carrying him.

❖ ❖ ❖

Doreen: Why does that letter bring tears to your eyes?

Duncan: Search me.

Doreen: It's written on onion skin.

23

Wilma & Wesley

Wilma: What do you say to a boomerang on its birthday?
Wesley: I have no clue.
Wilma: Many happy returns.

❖ ❖ ❖

Wilma: What dog is the best flyer?
Wesley: Beats me.
Wilma: An Airedale.

❖ ❖ ❖

Wilma: What starts with E and ends with E and has one letter in it?

Wesley: I have no idea.
Wilma: An envelope.

Wilma: What would happen if you fed your dog garlic and onions?
Wesley: You tell me.
Wilma: His bark would be worse than his bite.

Wilma: What do you call fear of tight chimneys?
Wesley: Who knows?
Wilma: Santa Claus-trophobia.

Wilma: What's a sheep's favorite snack?
Wesley: You've got me.
Wilma: A baa-loney sandwich.

❖   ❖   ❖

Wilma: What do you call a kitten that cheats on a test?
Wesley: My mind is blank.
Wilma: A copycat.

❖ ❖ ❖

Wilma: What creature is smarter than a talking parrot?
Wesley: That's a mystery.
Wilma: A spelling bee.

❖ ❖ ❖

Wilma: What's the best thing to do for fallen arches?
Wesley: I don't know.
Wilma: Pick them up.

24

Carter & Clara

Carter: What fairy-tale character hasn't done his ironing in years?
Clara: I have no clue.
Carter: Wrinkle Stiltzkin.

Carter: I went to the doctor and told him I tend to get fat in certain places.
Clara: What did he say?
Carter: Keep away from those places.

Carter: Who writes nursery rhymes and

squeezes oranges?

Clara: I can't guess.

Carter: Mother Juice.

Carter: I'm on my way to visit my outlaws.

Clara: You mean your in-laws, don't you?

Carter: No—outlaws. They're a bunch of bandits.

Carter: My wife writes me that she is all unstrung. What shall I do?

Clara: You tell me.

Carter: Maybe I should send her a wire.

Carter: I broke my nose in two places.

Clara: You better stay out of those places.

Carter: I lost my dog and I feel awful.

Clara: You must be terrier stricken.

Carter: I got my dog a flea collar.
Clara: Did he like it?
Carter: No. It ticked him off.

Carter: I have ringing in my ears. What should I do?
Clara: Maybe you should consider getting an unlisted ear.

Carter: I'm going to put you on bread and water as punishment. How would you like that?
Clara: I would like the whole wheat toasted.

Carter: I once shot a lion 15 feet long.
Clara: Some lying!

25

More Did You Hear?

Do you know what Mr. Goodyear is doing now?
He is re-tired.

❖   ❖   ❖

Did you hear about the kid who was 20 minutes early for school?
He was in a class by himself.

❖   ❖   ❖

Did you hear about the artist with a poor memory?
He kept drawing a blank.

83

Did you hear the story about the bed?

It was just made up.

Did you hear about the guy who stole the judge's calendar?

He got 12 months.

Did you hear about the shoplifter at the lingerie shop?

She gave police the slip.

Did you hear about the guy who had his whole left side shot off?

He's all right now.

Did you hear about the successful school play?

It was a class act.

Did you hear about the boardinghouse that blew up?

Roomers were flying.

Say, did you read in the newspaper about the fellow who ate six dozen pancakes at one sitting?

No, how waffle!

Did you know that Nancy married a janitor?

He just swept her off her feet.

Did your watch stop when it fell on the floor?

Sure. Did you think it would go right on through?

26

Ambrose & Agatha

Ambrose: What did the farmer say when he saw three ducks in his mailbox?
Agatha: I have no clue.
Ambrose: Bills, bills, bills.

❖   ❖   ❖

Ambrose: What happened to the two silk worms who had a race?
Agatha: Beats me.
Ambrose: They ended up in a tie.

❖   ❖   ❖

Ambrose: What is a navel destroyer?

Agatha: I can't guess.
Ambrose: A hula hoop with a nail in it.

Ambrose: What is white and lifts weights?
Agatha: I have no idea.
Ambrose: An extra-strength aspirin.

Ambrose: What did Humpty-Dumpty do after the fall?
Agatha: You tell me.
Ambrose: He called his lawyer.

Ambrose: What does a pig put on himself when he gets a sunburn?
Agatha: I give up.
Ambrose: Oinkment.

Ambrose: What job does a loon do in the forest?
Agatha: Who knows?
Ambrose: He's a loon ranger.

Ambrose: What does it take to be a plumber?
Agatha: You've got me.
Ambrose: Pipe dreams.

Ambrose: What fruit is always complaining?
Agatha: That's a mystery.
Ambrose: A crab apple.

27

Peggy & Paul

Peggy: How do you make a breadstick?
Paul: I have no clue.
Peggy: Use a lot of glue.

Peggy: How can you recognize a gypsy moth?
Paul: Beats me.
Peggy: It tries to tell your fortune.

Peggy: How many wheels does a car have?
Paul: I can't guess.
Peggy: Six, with the steering wheel and spare tire.

Peggy: How do hot dogs speak?
Paul: I have no idea.
Peggy: Frankly.

❖ ❖ ❖

Peggy: How did the prisoner escape?
Paul: You tell me.
Peggy: He broke out with the measles.

❖ ❖ ❖

Peggy: How did the dove save so much money?
Paul: I give up.
Peggy: By using coooo-pons.

❖ ❖ ❖

Peggy: How do you catch a unique bunny?
Paul: Who knows?
Peggy: Unique up on him.

❖ ❖ ❖

Peggy: How do you catch a tame bunny?
Paul: You've got me.
Peggy: The tame way.

❖ ❖ ❖

Peggy: How would you punctuate the sentence: "I saw a five-dollar bill on the sidewalk?"
Paul: My mind is blank.
Peggy: I'd make a dash after it.

❖ ❖ ❖

Peggy: How do you catch celery?
Paul: That's a mystery.
Peggy: You stalk it.

❖ ❖ ❖

Peggy: How did you get rid of the bloodhounds that were trailing us?
Paul: I threw a penny in the stream, and they followed the cent.

28

More Bible Fun

What was the name of Isaiah's horse?
Is Me. Isaiah said, "Woe, is me."

How were Adam and Eve prevented from gambling?
Their pair-o-dice was taken away from them.

What do you have that Cain, Abel, and Seth never had?
Grandparents.

❖ ❖ ❖

What simple affliction brought about the death of Samson?

Fallen arches.

❖ ❖ ❖

How were the Egyptians paid for goods taken by the Israelites when they fled from Egypt?

The Egyptians got a check on the bank of the Red Sea.

❖ ❖ ❖

When is high finance first mentioned in the Bible?

When Pharaoh's daughter took a little prophet from the bulrushes.

❖ ❖ ❖

Where is tennis mentioned in the Bible?

When Joseph served in Pharaoh's court.

❖ ❖ ❖

Where in the Bible does it suggest that men should wash dishes?

In 2 Kings 21:13—"And I will wipe Jerusalem

*as a man wipeth a dish, wiping it, and turning
it upside down."*

Paul the apostle was a great preacher and
teacher and earned his living as a tentmaker.
What other occupation did Paul have?

*He was a baker. We know this because he went
to Fill-a-pie.*

When did Moses sleep with five people in one
bed?

When he slept with his forefathers.

What did Adam and Eve do when they were
expelled from the Garden of Eden?

They raised Cain.

29

Eileen & Olivia

Eileen: How do you get rid of bedbugs?
Olivia: I have no clue.
Eileen: Make them sleep on the couch.

❖ ❖ ❖

Eileen: How do you make a kitchen sink?
Olivia: Beats me.
Eileen: Throw it in the ocean.

❖ ❖ ❖

Eileen: How can you tell if a lobster is fresh?
Olivia: I can't guess.
Eileen: If he tries to kiss you.

Eileen: How do you make a strawberry shake?

Olivia: I have no idea.

Eileen: Sneak up on it and say, "Boo!"

Eileen: How is the archaeologist doing?

Olivia: You tell me.

Eileen: Her life's work is in ruins.

Eileen: How much does it cost for an elephant to get a haircut?

Olivia: I give up.

Eileen: Five dollars for the haircut and five hundred dollars for the chair.

Eileen: How did you find the lost leopard?

Olivia: I just spotted him.

Eileen: How much sand would be in a hole one foot long, one foot wide, and one foot deep?

Olivia: You've got me.

Eileen: None, silly. There is no sand in a hole.

❖ ❖ ❖

Eileen: How do you keep a rhinoceros from charging?

Olivia: My mind is blank.

Eileen: Take away his credit card.

30

Rob & Rachel

Rob: Which is the bossiest type of ant?
Rachel: I have no clue.
Rob: Tyrant.

❖ ❖ ❖

Rob: Which ant is an army officer?
Rachel: Beats me.
Rob: Sergeant.

❖ ❖ ❖

Rob: Who sells ice cream in Arizona?
Rachel: I can't guess.
Rob: Good Yuma man.

❖ ❖ ❖

Rob: Where was Captain Kidd's chest buried?
Rachel: I have no idea.
Rob: With the rest of his body.

❖ ❖ ❖

Rob: Where do they keep the kettle on a ship?
Rachel: You tell me.
Rob: In the boiler room.

❖ ❖ ❖

Rob: Where do you buy a comb?
Rachel: I give up.
Rob: At a parts store.

❖ ❖ ❖

Rob: Where does Saint Nick go on holidays?
Rachel: Who knows?
Rob: On a Santa Cruz.

❖ ❖ ❖

Rob: Where do they keep all the pigs in Oregon?
Rachel: You've got me.
Rob: In the state pen.

Rob: Where does a cow go on Saturday night?
Rachel: My mind is blank.
Rob: To the moo-vies.

Rob: Where do you learn how to scoop ice cream?
Rachel: That's a mystery.
Rob: At sundae school.

Rob: Where is the place where part of the family waits until the others are through with the car.
Rachel: I don't know.
Rob: Home.

Rob: When are roads unpleasant?
Rachel: Search me.
Rob: When they are crossroads.

Rob: When is a car like a frog?

Rachel: I don't have the foggiest.
Rob: When it's being toad.

Rob: When Big Chief Shortcake died, what did his widow do?
Rachel: I'm in the dark.
Rob: Squaw bury Shortcake.

31

Stop that Knocking

Knock, knock.
Who's there?
Radio.
Radio who?
Radio not—here I come.

❖ ❖ ❖

Knock, knock.
Who's there?
Toodle.
Toodle who?
Toodle who to you, too!

❖ ❖ ❖

Knock, knock.
Who's there?
Barbie.
Barbie who?
Barbie Q Chicken.

❖   ❖   ❖

Knock, knock.
Who's there?
Noah.
Noah who?
Noah good place to eat?

❖   ❖   ❖

Knock, knock.
Who's there?
Roach.
Roach who?
Roach you a letter, did you get it?

❖   ❖   ❖

Knock, knock.
Who's there?
Carmen.
Carmen who?
Carmen to my parlor, said the spider to the fly.

❖ ❖ ❖

Knock, knock.
Who's there?
Altoona.
Altoona who?
Altoona piano and you play it.

❖ ❖ ❖

Knock, knock.
Who's there?
House.
House who?
House it going?

❖ ❖ ❖

Knock, knock.
Who's there?
Lettuce.
Lettuce who?
Lettuce discuss this like mature adults.

❖ ❖ ❖

Knock, knock.
Who's there?
Albee.
Albee who?
Albee a monkey's uncle!

❖   ❖   ❖

Knock, knock.
Who's there?
Wanda.
Wanda who?
Wanda come out and play?

32

Art & Bart

Art: What do you say to a king who falls off his chair?
Bart: I have no clue.
Art: Throne for a loop?

Art: What did the dog say when someone grabbed his tail?
Bart: Beats me.
Art: That's the end of me!

Art: What do you call a baby who is learning to talk?

Bart: I can't guess.
Art: A little word processor.

❖ ❖ ❖

Art: What do you do with all the fruit that grows around here?
Bart: Well, we eat what we can—and what we can't, we can!

❖ ❖ ❖

Art: What did the baked potato say to the cook?
Bart: You tell me.
Art: Foiled again!

❖ ❖ ❖

Art: What do you get if your stockings fall off, your ornaments break, and Santa tracks soot through your living room?
Bart: I give up.
Art: A merry Chris-mess.

❖ ❖ ❖

Art: What does a king drink when he doesn't like coffee.
Bart: Who knows?
Art: Royal-tea.

❖ ❖ ❖

Art: What did the baby banana say to the mother banana?
Bart: You've got me.
Art: I don't peel good.

❖ ❖ ❖

Art: What do you call a bear who cries a lot?
Bart: My mind is blank.
Art: Winnie the Boo-hoo.

❖ ❖ ❖

Art: What do you call little bugs that live on the moon?
Bart: That's a mystery.
Art: Luna ticks.

33

Pam & Melba

Pam: How does a hobo travel?
Melba: I have no clue.
Pam: On a tramp steamer.

❖ ❖ ❖

Pam: How come you don't answer the door?
Melba: It never asks any questions.

❖ ❖ ❖

Pam: How did your horse farm turn out?
Melba: Terrible. I planted the horses too deep.

❖ ❖ ❖

Pam: How is the astronomer doing?
Melba: Things are looking up.

Pam: How did the ex-convict get a job at the music store?
Melba: You tell me.
Pam: Not too well, they found out he had a record.

Pam: How do bees get to school?
Melba: I give up.
Pam: They wait at the buzz stop.

Pam: How did you know the frog was sick?
Melba: You've got me.
Pam: He toad me.

Pam: How did the comedian like his eggs?
Melba: My mind is blank.
Pam: Funny side up.

Pam: How do you paint a rabbit?
Melba: That's a mystery.
Pam: With hare spray.

34

Daffy Definitions

Circle: A round line with a hole in the middle.

❖   ❖   ❖

Editor: A literary barber.

❖   ❖   ❖

Mischief: The Chief's daughter.

❖   ❖   ❖

Nursery: Bawlroom.

❖   ❖   ❖

Punctuality: The best way to avoid meeting people.

Quadruplets: Four crying out loud.

Screen door: Something the kids get a bang out of.

Shopper: Someone who likes to go buy-buy.

Spanking: Stern punishment.

35

Barnaby & Barbie

Barnaby: Why do people stand on two legs?
Barbie: I have no clue.
Barnaby: If they didn't, they would fall over.

Barnaby: Why did the two fish get married?
Barbie: Beats me.
Barnaby: Because they were hooked on each other.

Barnaby: Why was the lifeguard at the store?
Barbie: I can't guess.

Barnaby: He heard he could save a lot.

Barnaby: Why is it never good to swim on an empty stomach?
Barbie: I have no idea.
Barnaby: Because it's easier to swim in water.

Barnaby: Why are you so mad?
Barbie: I brought my leopard-skin coat to the cleaners.
Barnaby: What's wrong with that?
Barbie: It came back spotless.

Barnaby: Why didn't the elephant buy a small sports car?
Barbie: I give up.
Barnaby: It had no trunk space.

Barnaby: How did the carpenter break all his teeth?
Barbie: Who knows?

Barnaby: From chewing his nails.

Barnaby: Why did the seal cross the road?
Barbie: You've got me.
Barnaby: To get to the otter side.

Barnaby: Why didn't the kitchen window like the living room window?
Barbie: My mind is blank.
Barnaby: Because it was such a big pane.

Barnaby: Why was the weatherman arrested?
Barbie: That's a mystery.
Barnaby: For shooting the breeze.

Barnaby: Why did the rooster refuse to fight?
Barbie: I don't know.
Barnaby: He was chicken.

36

Lola & Lionel

Lola: Which is the dumbest ant?
Lionel: I have no clue.
Lola: Ignorant.

❖ ❖ ❖

Lola: Which is the biggest ant?
Lionel: Beats me.
Lola: Elephant.

❖ ❖ ❖

Lola: Which rabbit stole from the rich to give to the poor?
Lionel: I can't guess.
Lola: Rabbit Hood.

❖ ❖ ❖

Lola: Where does a skunk sit in church?
Lionel: I have no idea.
Lola: In a pew.

❖ ❖ ❖

Lola: Where do you go to become a smart prisoner?
Lionel: Who knows?
Lola: Go directly to Yale.

❖ ❖ ❖

Lola: Where does a track star keep his money?
Lionel: You've got me.
Lola: In a pole vault.

❖ ❖ ❖

Lola: Where is Captain Hook's treasure chest?
Lionel: My mind is blank.
Lola: Under his treasure shirt.

❖ ❖ ❖

Lola: Where does the king keep his army?

Lionel: That's a mystery.
Lola: Up his sleeve-y.

❖   ❖   ❖

Lola: Where do rabbits go when they get married?
Lionel: I don't know.
Lola: On their bunnymoon.

❖   ❖   ❖

Lola: Where was the first french fry made?
Lionel: Search me.
Lola: In Greece.

❖   ❖   ❖

Lola: When is the best time for a farmer to retire?
Lionel: I don't have the foggiest.
Lola: About nine o'clock.

❖   ❖   ❖

Lola: When is an operation funny?
Lionel: I'm in the dark.
Lola: When it leaves the patient in stitches.

❖   ❖   ❖

Lola: When rain falls, does it ever get up again?

Lionel: You've got me guessing.

Lola: Oh, yes—in dew time.

37

Bertram & Bernard

Bertram: What do you call 300 rabbits marching backward?
Bernard: I have no clue.
Bertram: A receding hareline.

❖   ❖   ❖

Bertram: What do you call a tire salesman?
Bernard: Beats me.
Bertram: A wheeler-dealer.

❖   ❖   ❖

Bertram: What is a musician's favorite dessert?

Bernard: I can't guess.
Bertram: Cello.

Bertram: What is the auto parts store slogan?
Bernard: I have no idea.
Bertram: You deserve a brake today.

Bertram: What did the police say when a famous drawing was stolen?
Bernard: You tell me.
Bertram: Details are sketchy.

Bertram: What has a long neck, a well-known name, and wears a cap?
Bernard: I give up.
Bertram: A bottle.

Bertram: What did the barber call his son?
Bernard: Who knows?
Bertram: A little shaver.

❖ ❖ ❖

Bertram: What goes tock-tick?
Bernard: You've got me.
Bertram: A backward clock.

❖ ❖ ❖

Bertram: What did the coffee say to the police?
Bernard: My mind is blank.
Bertram: I've been mugged.

❖ ❖ ❖

Bertram: What do you say to curtains?
Bernard: That's a mystery.
Bertram: Pull yourself together.

38

More Bible Riddles

In what place did the cock crow so that all the world could hear him?

On Noah's ark.

Where do you think the Israelites may have deposited their money?

At the banks of the Jordan.

What was the most expensive meal served in the Bible, and who ate it?

Esau. It cost him his birthright—Genesis 25:34.

❖   ❖   ❖

Why did Noah have to punish and discipline the chickens on the ark?

Because they were using "fowl" language.

❖   ❖   ❖

Why was Job always cold in bed?

Because he had such miserable comforters.

❖   ❖   ❖

What are the only wages that do not have any deductions?

The wages of sin.

❖   ❖   ❖

What were the Phoenicians famous for?

Blinds.

❖   ❖   ❖

Where did Noah strike the first nail in the ark?

On the head.

zebra with narrow stripes. Their first son had
no stripes. What did they call him?

Eutychus: Beats me.

Ichabod: Howard.

❖ ❖ ❖

Ichabod: What is the main ingredient of dog
biscuits?

Eutychus: You tell me.

Ichabod: Collie-flour.

❖ ❖ ❖

Ichabod: If a skunk got its nose cut off, how
would it smell?

Eutychus: I don't know.

Ichabod: As bad as ever.

❖ ❖ ❖

Ichabod: Is the joker animal, vegetable, or
mineral?

Eutychus: I can't guess.

Ichabod: Vegetable . . . he's a human bean.

❖ ❖ ❖

Ichabod: Where do giant condors come from?

Eutychus: I have no idea.

Ichabod: Eggs.

Ichabod: Where did the joker wind up for stealing shellfish?
Eutychus: I give up.
Ichabod: Small clams court.

❖ ❖ ❖

Ichabod: Where does the joker fill his car's gas tank?
Eutychus: Who knows?
Ichabod: At the villain station.

❖ ❖ ❖

Ichabod: When is it proper to go to bed with your shoes on?
Eutychus: You've got me.
Ichabod: When you are a horse.

❖ ❖ ❖

Ichabod: When is a horse not a horse?
Eutychus: That's a mystery.
Ichabod: When he turns into a barn.

❖ ❖ ❖

Ichabod: Who is safe when a man-eating tiger is loose?

Eutychus: I'm a blank.
Ichabod: Women and children.

Ichabod: Did you ever see a catfish?
Eutychus: No, but I saw a horsefly.

Ichabod: Did you hear about the cat who swallowed the duck?
Eutychus: It's unknown to me.
Ichabod: She became a duck-filled fatty-puss.

Ichabod: Did you hear about the cat who swallowed the ball of yarn?
Eutychus: I'm in the dark.
Ichabod: She had mittens.

Ichabod: Did you like the story about the dog who ran two miles just to pick up a stick?
Eutychus: No, I thought it was a little far-fetched!

Open the Door!

Knock, knock.
Who's there?
Waterloo.
Waterloo who?
Waterloo doing for dinner?

❖ ❖ ❖

Knock, knock.
Who's there?
Hollywood.
Hollywood who?
Hollywood be here if she could!

❖ ❖ ❖

Knock, knock.
Who's there?
Whittier.
Whittier who?
Whittier people always tell knock-knock
jokes!

❖   ❖   ❖

Knock, knock.
Who's there?
John.
John who?
John you marks, get set, go!

❖   ❖   ❖

Knock, knock.
Who's there?
Esther.
Esther who?
Esther a doctor in the house?

❖   ❖   ❖

Knock, knock.
Who's there?
Canoe.
Canoe who?
Canoe come out and play with me?

❖ ❖ ❖

Knock, knock.
Who's there?
Hannah.
Hannah who?
Hannah over all your money. This is a stick-up!

❖ ❖ ❖

Knock, knock.
Who's there?
China.
China who?
China cold out, isn't it?

❖ ❖ ❖

Knock, knock.
Who's there?
Kenya.
Kenya who?
Kenya open the door?

❖ ❖ ❖

Knock, knock.
Who's there?
Ghana.

Ghana who?
Ghana make you laugh!

❖ ❖ ❖

Knock, knock.
Who's there?
April.
April who?
April showers.

❖ ❖ ❖

Knock, knock.
Who's there?
Eric.
Eric who?
Eric conditioner.

❖ ❖ ❖

Knock, knock.
Who's there?
Witless.
Witless who?
Witless ring I thee wed.

❖ ❖ ❖

Knock, knock.
Who's There?

You.
You who?
Are you calling me?

❖ ❖ ❖

Knock, knock.
Who's there?
Hugh Maid.
Hugh Maid who?
Hugh Maid your bed, now lie in it!

❖ ❖ ❖

Knock, Knock.
Who's There?
Tacoma.
Tacoma who?
Tacoma all this way and you don't recognize me!

❖ ❖ ❖

Knock, knock.
Who's there?
Telly.
Telly who?
Telly scope.

❖ ❖ ❖

water?
  Lois: Beats me.
  Levi: It was planted in the spring.

❖ ❖ ❖

  Levi: Why did the man have to go to the hos
pital after a tomato fell on his head?
  Lois: You tell me.
  Levi: It was in a can.

❖ ❖ ❖

  Levi: Why did the dog run in circles?
  Lois: My mind is a blank.
  Levi: He was a watchdog and needed winding.

❖ ❖ ❖

  Levi: Why do elephants have ivory tusks?
  Lois: I can't guess.
  Levi: Iron ones would rust.

❖ ❖ ❖

  Levi: Why does a dog wag his tail?
  Lois: I have no idea.
  Levi: Nobody will wag it for him.

❖ ❖ ❖

138

Levi: Why did the boy stand behind the donkey?

Lois: I give up.

Levi: He thought he would get a kick out of it.

Levi: Why don't elephants play basketball?

Lois: Who knows?

Levi: They can't buy round sneakers.

Levi: Why did the farmer feed his sheep chunks of steel?

Lois: You've got me.

Levi: He wanted them to grow steel wool.

Levi: Why are wolves like cards?

Lois: That's a mystery.

Levi: They come in packs.

Levi: Why do giraffes have such long necks?

Lois: I'm a blank.

Levi: To connect their heads to their bodies.

139

Levi: Why couldn't the pony talk?
Lois: I don't have the foggiest.
Levi: He was a little horse.

Levi: Why are leopards spotted?
Lois: It's unknown to me.
Levi: So you can tell them from fleas.

Levi: Why did Santa have only seven rein-deer on Christmas Eve?
Lois: I'm in the dark.
Levi: Comet was home cleaning the sink.

Levi: Why did the kangaroo go to the doctor?
Lois: Search me.
Levi: He wasn't feeling jumpy anymore.

❖ ❖ ❖

Levi: Why does the joker go to bed with 50 cents every night?
Lois: I pass.

Levi: They're his sleeping quarters.

❖ ❖ ❖

Levi: Why doesn't the joker use mothballs to get rid of moths?
Lois: I don't know.
Levi: He can't aim those tiny mothballs to hit the moths.

❖ ❖ ❖

Levi: Why did the joker brush his teeth with gunpowder?
Lois: I have no clue.
Levi: He wanted to shoot his mouth off.

42

Show Me!

Show me a swine, and I'll show you hogwash.

❖ ❖ ❖

Show me a burned-out post office, and I'll show you a case of blackmail.

❖ ❖ ❖

Show me where Stalin is buried, and I'll show you a Communist plot.

❖ ❖ ❖

Show me a cross between a cannon and a

bell, and I'll show you a boomerang.

Show me a toddler caught playing in the mud, and I'll show you grime and punishment.

Show me a stolen sausage, and I'll show you a missing link.

Show me a gang of beggars, and I'll show you a ragtime band.

Show me a man who's afraid of Christmas, and I'll show you a Noel Coward.

Show me a frog on a lily pad, and I'll show you a toadstool.

Show me an arrogant insect, and I'll show

you a cocky roach.

Show me a man convicted of two crimes, and I'll show you a compound sentence.

Show me the first president's dentures, and I'll show you the George Washington Bridge.

Show me a squirrel's nest, and I'll show you the Nutcracker Suite.

Show me a cat that just ate a lemon, and I'll show you a sourpuss.

Show me a pharaoh who ate crackers in bed, and I'll show you a crumy mummy.

Show me Santa's helpers, and I'll show you

subordinate clauses.

Show me a girl who shuns the miniskirt, and
I'll show you hemlock.

43

Cyrus & Cornelia

Cyrus: What was the turtle doing on the free-way?
Cornelia: I have no clue.
Cyrus: About half a mile an hour.

❖ ❖ ❖

Cyrus: What kind of hawk has no wings?
Cornelia: I don't know.
Cyrus: A tomahawk.

❖ ❖ ❖

Cyrus: What did the pelican say when he caught a large fish?

146

Cornelia: Beats me.
Cyrus: This sure fills the bill.

Cyrus: What do you get if you cross a potato with an onion?
Cornelia: You tell me.
Cyrus: A potato with watery eyes.

Cyrus: What should you do with a dog who is eating a dictionary?
Cornelia: My mind is a blank.
Cyrus: Take the words right out of his mouth.

Cyrus: What sort of story did the peacock tell?
Cornelia: I can't guess.
Cyrus: A big tale.

Cyrus: What animals are always with you?
Cornelia: I have no idea.
Cyrus: A pair of calves.

Cyrus: What animal is a tattletale?
Cornelia: I give up.
Cyrus: The pig always squeals on you.

Cyrus: What is green, then purple, then green, then purple?
Cornelia: Who knows?
Cyrus: A pickle that works part-time as a grape.

Cyrus: What animal is the best baseball player?
Cornelia: You've got me.
Cyrus: The bat.

Cyrus: What is a monkey that eats potato chips called?
Cornelia: That's a mystery.
Cyrus: A chip monk.

Cyrus: What would you get if you crossed a porcupine and a skunk?
Cornelia: I'm a blank.
Cyrus: A smelly pincushion.

❖ ❖ ❖

Cyrus: What must a lion tamer know to teach a lion tricks?
Cornelia: I don't have the foggiest.
Cyrus: More than the lion.

❖ ❖ ❖

Cyrus: What did the beaver say to the tree?
Cornelia: It's unknown to me.
Cyrus: It's been nice gnawing you.

❖ ❖ ❖

Cyrus: What do hippopotamuses have that no other animals have?
Cornelia: I'm in the dark.
Cyrus: Baby hippos.

❖ ❖ ❖

Cyrus: What makes more noise than an angry lion?
Cornelia: Search me.
Cyrus: Two angry lions.

❖ ❖ ❖

Cyrus: What would you get if you crossed a laughing hyena and a cat?

Cornelia: I pass.
Cyrus: A giggle puss.

Cyrus: What is the highest form of animal life?
Cornelia: I don't know.
Cyrus: A giraffe.

Cyrus: What should you do if you find a gorilla asleep in your bed?
Cornelia: I have no clue.
Cyrus: Sleep somewhere else.

44

Rufus & Rachel

Rufus: What is an important aid in good grooming for pet mice?
Rachel: I have no clue.
Rufus: Mouse wash.

❖ ❖ ❖

Rufus: What did the mama broom and the papa broom say to the baby broom?
Rachel: I don't know.
Rufus: Go to sweep.

❖ ❖ ❖

Rufus: What do you get when you cross a

camel with the town dump?
  Rachel: Beats me.
  Rufus: Humpty-Dumpty.

Rufus: What fish is man's best friend?
Rachel: You tell me.
Rufus: The dogfish.

Rufus: What beans won't grow from seeds?
Rachel: My mind is a blank.
Rufus: Jelly beans.

Rufus: What fish goes boating?
Rachel: I can't guess.
Rufus: A sailfish.

Rufus: What do teenage boy gorillas do when
they see pretty teenage girl gorillas?
  Rachel: I have no idea.
  Rufus: They go ape.

Rufus: What kind of dog can fly?
Rachel: I give up.
Rufus: A bird dog.

Rufus: What animal eats with its tail?
Rachel: Who knows?
Rufus: All animals do. They also sleep with them.

Rufus: What is gray, has four legs, and weighs 98 pounds?
Rachel: You've got me.
Rufus: A fat mouse.

Rufus: What did the dog's right eye say to his left eye?
Rachel: I'm a blank.
Rufus: Just between us, something smells.

Rufus: What do you call a meeting among many dogs?
Rachel: I don't have the foggiest.

Rufus: A bowwow powwow.

Rufus: What do dogs always take on their camping trips?
Rachel: It's unknown to me.
Rufus: Pup tents.

Rufus: What did the dog say when it got its tail caught in the door?
Rachel: Search me.
Rufus: It won't be long now!

Rufus: What was the first cat to fly?
Rachel: I pass.
Rufus: Kitty Hawk.

Rufus: What did the joker get when he crossed poison ivy with a four-leaf clover?
Rachel: I don't know.
Rufus: A rash of good luck.

Rufus: What would you get if you crossed a cat and a pair of galoshes?

Rachel: I have no clue.

Rufus: Puss n' boots.

Rufus: What is yellow and always points north?

Rachel: Beats me.

Rufus: A magnetic banana.

45

Stop that Knocking

Knock, knock.
Who's there?
Hosea.
Hosea who?
Hosea can you see?

❖ ❖ ❖

Knock, knock.
Who's there?
Milt.
Milt who?
Milt the cow.

❖ ❖ ❖

Knock, knock.
Who's there?
Manila.
Manila who?
Manila ice cream!

❖ ❖ ❖

Knock, knock.
Who's there?
Easter.
Easter who?
Easter anybody home?

❖ ❖ ❖

Knock, knock.
Who's there?
Luke.
Luke who?
Luke both ways before crossing.

❖ ❖ ❖

Knock, knock.
Who's there?
Carrie.
Carrie who?
Carrie me inside, I'm tired.

❖ ❖ ❖

Knock, knock.
Who's there?
Luke.
Luke who?
Luke through the keyhole and see.

❖ ❖ ❖

Knock, knock.
Who's there?
Ken.
Ken who?
Ken't you guess?

❖ ❖ ❖

Knock, knock.
Who's there?
Dill.
Dill who?
Big Dill!

❖ ❖ ❖

Knock, Knock.
Who's there?
Archer.
Archer who?
Archer glad to see me?

❖ ❖ ❖

Knock, knock.
Who's there?
Cologne.
Cologne who?
Cologne Ranger!

❖ ❖ ❖

Knock, knock.
Who's there?
Yukon.
Yukon who?
Yukon too many people!

❖ ❖ ❖

Knock, knock.
Who's there?
Amnesia.
Amnesia who?
Oh, I see you have it, too!

❖ ❖ ❖

Knock, knock.
Who's there?
Canoe.
Canoe who?
Canoe please get off my foot?

❖ ❖ ❖

Knock, knock.
Who's there?
Tuna.
Tuna who?
Tuna to a disco station!

❖ ❖ ❖

Knock, knock.
Who's there?
Sarah.
Sarah who?
Sarah echo in here?

❖ ❖ ❖

Knock, knock.
Who's there?
Saul.
Saul who?
Saul in your head!

❖ ❖ ❖

Knock, knock.
Who's there?
Lotto.
Lotto who?
Lotto good that will do.

❖   ❖   ❖

Knock, knock.
Who's there?
Mayonnaise.
Mayonnaise who?
Mayonnaise have seen the glory of the coming
of the Lord . . .

46

Abner & Abigail

Abner: How can you recognize a dogwood tree?
Abigail: I have no clue.
Abner: By its bark.

❖ ❖ ❖

Abner: How do you scold an elephant?
Abigail: I don't know.
Abner: Say tusk tusk.

❖ ❖ ❖

Abner: How can you stop a dog from barking in the backyard?

Abigail: Beats me.
Abner: Put him in the front yard.

Abner: How do you get fur from a bear?
Abigail: You tell me.
Abner: Run fast in the opposite direction.

Abner: How do you move in a crowd of porcupines?
Abigail: My mind is a blank.
Abner: Very carefully.

Abner: How did the joker make a hotdog shiver?
Abigail: I can't guess.
Abner: He covered it with chili beans.

Abner: How does the joker file an ax?
Abigail: I have no idea.
Abner: Under the letter A.

Abner: How did the joker eat a computer?
Abigail: I give up.
Abner: Bit by bit.

Abner: How does the joker make a banana split?
Abigail: Who knows?
Abner: He cuts it in half.

Abner: How did the joker fit a rhinoceros into his car?
Abigail: You've got me.
Abner: He made one of the elephants get out.

47

Famous Sayings

What did the sailor say?
Knot bad.

❖ ❖ ❖

What did the drummer say?
It's hard to beat.

❖ ❖ ❖

What did the coffee salesman say?
It's a grind.

❖ ❖ ❖

What did the demolition worker say?
Smashing!

❖ ❖ ❖

What did the dressmaker say?
Just sew-sew.

❖ ❖ ❖

What did the astronomer say?
Things are looking up.

❖ ❖ ❖

What did the street cleaner say?
Things are picking up.

❖ ❖ ❖

What did the gunsmith say?
Booming!

❖ ❖ ❖

What did the botanist say?
Everything's coming up roses.

❖ ❖ ❖

What did the pianist say?
Right on key.

❖   ❖   ❖

What did the deep-sea diver say?
I'm about to go under.

❖   ❖   ❖

What did the floor waxer say?
Going smoothly.

❖   ❖   ❖

What did the zookeeper say?
It's beastly!

❖   ❖   ❖

What did the teacher say?
My work is classy.

❖   ❖   ❖

What did the gravedigger say?
Monumental!

❖   ❖   ❖

What did the iceman say?
Not so hot.

❖ ❖ ❖

What did the counterfeiter say?
We're forging on.

❖ ❖ ❖

What did the counterman say?
Pretty crummy.

❖ ❖ ❖

What did the dairy farmer say?
Cheesy, in a whey.

❖ ❖ ❖

What did the baker say?
I've been making a lot of dough lately.

❖ ❖ ❖

What did the tree surgeon say?
I've some shady deals going.

❖ ❖ ❖

168

What did the pilot say?
Pretty much up in the air.

What did the photographer say?
Everything is clicking and developing well.

What did the locksmith say?
Everything's opening up.

What did the musician say?
Nothing of note has been happening.

48

Claud & Chloe

Claud: What song does the mean man sing at Christmastime?

Chloe: I have no clue.

Claud: "Deck the halls with poison ivy, fa la la la la . . ."

Claud: What does the computer eat for lunch?

Chloe: I don't know.

Claud: Floppy Joes and microchips.

Claud: What would you get if you crossed a puppy with a mean boy?

Chloe: Beats me.

Claud: A bully dog.

❖   ❖   ❖

Claud: What would you get if you crossed a pit bull and a cow?

Chloe: You tell me.

Claud: An animal that's too mean to milk.

❖   ❖   ❖

Claud: What did the joker get when he put his dog in the bathtub?

Chloe: My mind is a blank.

Claud: Ring around the collie.

❖   ❖   ❖

Claud: What does the joker call a man who shaves 20 times a day?

Chloe: I can't guess.

Claud: A barber.

❖   ❖   ❖

Claud: What did the joker get when he crossed a swimming pool with a movie theater?

Chloe: I have no idea.
Claud: A dive-in movie.

Claud: What happened when the joker robbed the hamburger factory?
Chloe: I give up.
Claud: Things came to a grinding halt.

Claud: What goes A B C D E F G H I J K L M N O P Q R S T U V W X Y Z slurp?
Chloe: Who knows?
Claud: The boy eating a bowl of alphabet soup.

❖ ❖ ❖

Claud: What's black and white and goes around and around?
Chloe: You've got me.
Claud: A penguin in a revolving door.

❖ ❖ ❖

Claud: What did the boy get when he crossed a string quartet with a chocolate dessert?
Chloe: That's a mystery.
Claud: Cello pudding.

❖ ❖ ❖

Claud: What do you call a man who bites a policeman?
Chloe: I'm a blank.
Claud: A law a-biting citizen.

❖ ❖ ❖

Claud: What did the man get when he crossed some cabbage with a tiger?
Chloe: I don't have the foggiest.
Claud: Man-eating coleslaw.

❖ ❖ ❖

Claud: What kind of a waiter never accepts a tip?
Chloe: I'm in the dark.
Claud: A dumbwaiter.

❖ ❖ ❖

Claud: What's black and white and hides in a cave?
Chloe: Search me.
Claud: A zebra that owes money.

Claud: What kind of water can't be frozen?
Chloe: I pass.
Claud: Boiling water.

❖   ❖   ❖

Claud: What did the man get when he dialed
555-273859361394364737 on his phone?
Chloe: I don't know.
Claud: A blister on his finger.

❖   ❖   ❖

Claud: What does the joker fill his car with?
Chloe: I have no clue.
Claud: Laughing gas.